Pray W

Family, friends, fears about the future, the widening gap between rich and poor — these are some of the concerns expressed in this collection of prayers. Based on prayers written by Kenyan students, they will echo the thoughts of others throughout the world who are trying to relate their faith to life today.

Woven into the prayers is an outlook that is essentially African — an awareness of God's presence in every part of life and a joyfulness and delight in his creation. Whether used in private or in public worship, these prayers will give new insights into how to pray for ourselves and for each other.

To my former students of Limuru Girls' School, in 1973–1980,
to whom I owe the inspiration for this book.

PRAY WITH US

Maureen Edwards

A LION PAPERBACK
Tring · Belleville · Sydney

Copyright © 1984 Maureen Edwards

Published by
Lion Publishing plc
Icknield Way, Tring, Herts, England
ISBN 0 85648 710 4
Lion Publishing Corporation
10885 Textile Road, Belleville, Michigan 48111, USA
ISBN 0 85648 710 4
Albatross Books
PO Box 320, Sutherland, NSW 2232, Australia
ISBN 0 86760 509 X

British Library Cataloguing in Publication Data

Edwards, Maureen
    Pray with us.
    1. Youth – Prayer-books and devotions
    I. Title
    242'.83   BV283.Y6

    ISBN 0–85648–710–4

Printed and bound in Great Britain by
Collins, Glasgow.

Contents

Acknowledgements

I would like to express appreciation to the students of the following schools who so eagerly contributed ideas:

Limuru Girls' School; Loreto High School, Limuru; Alliance Boys' School, Kikuyu; Ribe Secondary School; Meru School; Kaaga High School; Kaaga Harambee Secondary School; Kithirune Secondary School; Mukumu Girls' School, and Meru Teachers' College.

I would also like to thank Mrs W. Mwangi, Sister Germaine, Mrs H. Nyagah, Mrs E. Elson, the Revd F. Welch, Father Sharkey, the Revd Elizabeth Bellamy and the Revd Colin Dundon for their help and encouragement.

Introduction

Here is a book of prayers and meditations from young
Kenyan Christians. The idea began at Limuru Girls'
School where I tried to encourage students to contribute
to prayers in the school service each Sunday morning.
Then I collected more ideas from students in other
secondary schools in different parts of Kenya. The
thought of almost every line of every prayer has come
from them, though the language is edited to create units
of prayer that can be read in worship. Many lines are
similar to the kind of prayers that all Christians pray
throughout the world; others are essentially African and
reflect a deep awareness of the presence of God in every
part of life. Some prayers and meditations express doubts
and cynicism, for they come from young people who ask
questions and search for meaning and acceptance. They
include a growing sense of wonder as students learn more
of the complexities of God's creation and express a deep
concern for personal relationships and the great social,
political and ecological problems that face us all.

I hope this book will be used in two ways:
- Where we share the experience and concerns of Kenyan
  young people we can pray together with them.
- Where the thought is different from ours, these prayers
  become a mirror in which is reflected another way of
  life.

To approach God with the refreshing and different insights
of young people in another part of the world church
enriches us and creates a wider fellowship of prayer. My
own faith was deepened and widened by all that I learnt
from Kenyan Christians and I am profoundly thankful for
all that they taught me.

Maureen Edwards

Kenya 'Through the Looking Glass'

The prayers in this book reflect characteristics of Kenyan life. So a brief word of explanation is needed to help readers in other countries understand their background. African Christians are proud of their religious heritage and are seeking to relate their faith to their traditions. It is important for the non-African reader to be sensitive to this and keep an open mind on what follows in this section.

Awareness of God

Long before the coming of Christianity, African peoples were aware that beyond the powers of ancestors and spirits, there was one supreme God who created all and controlled all. He could not be seen or explained, but he was there. Those who lived around Mount Kenya associated his presence with the mountain and its mysterious snow-capped peaks, so often covered in cloud.

The Kikuyu called him Ngai; the Meru called him Murungu, and as they prayed they faced the sacred mountain. Earthquakes, storm, rain, thunder and lightning, were signs of his presence.

The Kambe said, 'God lives in the skies above; he makes everything grow by pouring rain. We call him "God of the rain".'

The Luo called him Were, 'father of grace'. Like a father in African family life, he was the wisest. He was the 'grandfather' of all people, who always existed and provided rain and fertile lands for his people. He was the source of all life.

All this was a preparation for the gospel when it was first proclaimed in East Africa 150 years ago and enabled people of all ages to respond to the call of Christ. Awareness of God's presence is strikingly characteristic of Kenyan Christians today. The God of whom they were already conscious through their traditions, has made himself known to them and has come to them in the person of Jesus Christ. Christ speaks to them, 'He who has seen me has seen the

Father.' They know, too, the indwelling presence of God as Holy Spirit.

Life After Death
Kenyan people have never thought of death as the end of life. Although death often cut short a happy, useful life in the community, according to traditional belief the spirit of the person remained alive to continue helping and protecting his family. The ancestors were called the 'living-dead'. The Duruma community believed that the ancestors rested in their graves during the day, but at night they wandered from place to place watching over their people. Sometimes they appeared to living members of the family in dreams. Kenyans never worshipped their ancestors but respected and sought to obey them. The ancestors were regarded as mediators through whom they could pray to the supreme God.

Kenyan Christians believe that these traditions find fulfilment in Christ who offers new life, a life which begins now and continues beyond death, and which links Christians today with all the redeemed, of every age and race.

Community
There are many ethnic communities within Kenya as in other African countries. Each community has its own customs, traditions and beliefs. There is above all a sense of 'togetherness' expressed in the national motto 'Harambee', meaning 'Let's all pull together.'

Some people tell stories of their origins. The Kikuyu tell of their great ancestors Gikuyu and Mumbi to whom Ngai gave the vast and fertile lands that lie to the west of Mount Kenya. The Meru tell of the prophet Mugwe who led their people out of the land of Mbwaa into the country that is now their home. Traditions like these fostered a sense of unity and solidarity, and so did the act of passing on stories and wise sayings from one generation to another.

In the rural community each person took his share of work and responsibility, and everyone was cared for. Amongst the Taita, when someone wanted to build a house he was helped by his relatives. The women collected the grass and the men collected the poles and sticks. In the past, the village usually consisted of the home of the chief or elder surrounded by the houses of his many relatives. The village was a family and it was often called by the title of the chief. In such surroundings the child was safe. Wherever he wandered there were members of the family who cared for him. In Taita villages the houses of the elders were built on slightly higher ground so that they could watch over the children.

In this context to steal, or commit adultery, or to quarrel was not merely an offence against the person involved; it broke the oneness of people. The evil man was hostile towards the community and his thoughts or words brought misfortune to them. He may have wished them ill or cursed them. The good man, on the other hand, was free from grudges, bitterness and witchcraft.

What of the community of Kenya today? In remote villages the old ways are still treasured; little has changed. Yet for most Kenyans it seems that the influences of Western life-styles and development have undermined their traditional values. Many, who have left home to live and work in the city, are unemployed, disillusioned, lonely and rejected. Many have turned to begging and thieving.

Most Kenyan young people live 'between two worlds', not knowing which way to go. They would like to restore all that was good, but the changes that are taking place around them are beyond their control. They appreciate the benefits of change and want a better standard of life for their children, but they do not want to throw away the rich heritage of their past.

Christ offers a new beginning: he invites us all to become members of a new community . . . the church. This community is not an ethnic group, but a community of faith for people of every race, colour and nationality. It does not depend on any one culture, but includes them all. Within this new community we are to make sure that we care for everyone and strive to build the kind of society in which no one is forced to turn to begging or crime to make a living.

Childhood and Family Life

There was always great rejoicing when a child was born.

13

Goats or sheep were slaughtered and a feast was held to celebrate another new beginning for the community. In Embu tradition, the new baby boy was taken out to the highway to receive a small bow and arrow, for he would become a man, protecting and providing for his family. If the baby was a girl, she would be given a little bundle of wood, to symbolize her future role to carry bundles of firewood on her back. The mother saved and treasured these small tokens of her child's value to the community.

Great care was taken to give the child a meaningful name. Often the child was called after his parents or grandparents. Among the Duruma, the father would take hold of his child's ear and give it a little shake, saying, 'Your name is . . . guard it and honour it.'

At a very early age children were expected to help the family. The boy became an 'apprentice' to his father and learnt to care for sheep and goats, carve wood or hunt. The girl helped to clean the house, fetched water and firewood and helped to look after the younger children.

Each evening, the family gathered round the fire, while the food was being cooked, to sing and tell stories. The child grew up wanting to imitate the courage and goodness of his ancestors whose brave deeds were told in word and song. Through imaginative and symbolic folk-tales he learnt to value wisdom, kindness and hard work and to despise meanness, deceit and laziness. Respect for parents and elders was never questioned. Children were reminded that they owed their parents everything.

The most important aspect of life which the child had to learn was the religious one. But religion, like other traditions, was not taught by formal instruction. From the moment of birth, the child was included in religious ceremonies and prayers. He was aware that his parents spoke to the spirits of his ancestors; he was aware of the presence of the supreme God, to whom they prayed and offered sacrifice. With reverence and awe he watched offerings of cereal and drink being poured into the sacred soil. With joy he shared the religious customs performed each time another baby was born. With growing interest he watched the religious customs which were part of initiation and marriage ceremonies. He was allowed to attend every

14

funeral and to see the body of the dead person. He knew that though the body was laid to rest, the spirit lived on.

The Bible, too, talks about respect for every member of the family and focusses our attention on Jesus, the Son of God, growing to manhood within the security of a Jewish family. In the midst of a busy life he found time for people and time for children; time for telling stories and time to listen. Whoever received a child in his name, received Christ himself. No child is too insignificant to be helped. True happiness depends not on the number or quality of our possessions but upon our willingness to serve one another.

Preparation for Marriage

As children entered their teens a special ceremony was held to initiate them into adult life. In most African communities boys, and sometimes girls, were circumcised, though after years of controversy girls are rarely expected to undergo this ordeal today. This was a great test of courage and the young person brought shame on his family if he flinched or cried out during the operation. It was a preparation for future situations when he would have to face danger and defend his family. Where circumcision was not practised, there was usually some other test of courage.

This was also a time for education for sex, marriage and family relationships. They were taught again the traditions of their people, the importance of respect for parents and elders and the particular duties they would have to perform in the community.

After the ceremony there was a feast and presents were given. This was a great moment: it was the end of childhood and the beginning of manhood. They were expected to exercise self-control and wisdom. The young man could now begin to own property, symbolized by the presents he received. Preparations could also be made for marriage.

In most communities, marriages were arranged by the parents or by a trusted relative. They knew best who would be faithful, kind and hard-working, and took great care to find the right person. Some communities, like the Kikuyu, allowed the young people themselves to choose a partner but the agreement of parents was always sought. Both fami-

15

lies met to discuss the bride-price. This was a gift from the bridegroom to the girl's family. It helped to compensate them for the loss of their daughter and it was a token of her value as a person.

Many other interesting customs were observed and this too was an occasion for feasting. Many Africans had more than one wife and sometimes a man's status in the community was estimated according to the size of his family. Within this large family, however, tasks were shared and there was a strict code of behaviour and faithfulness. High moral standards and self-control had been emphasized throughout initiation customs. Sex before marriage was forbidden, and the whole community despised and severely punished those who lowered their standards. Today, African marriage faces problems similar to those that are affecting family life in other changing societies throughout the world. Kenyan Christians realize the need to hold to the unchanging values of faithfulness and respect and also to emphasize the qualities of love and forgiveness which support a Christian marriage.

Fears

There was a saying amongst the Embu, 'A young man never dies unless he is poisoned.' Whatever the cause of death, the people believed that someone had wished him ill. Someone had cursed him and those words carried power to bring evil. Sometimes the community accused a childless wife, or a man who lived alone. Sometimes they had good reason to suspect a bitter, revengeful individual. Sometimes, however, innocent people were wrongly suspected, hunted out and put to death for witchcraft.

In other communities the ancestors were blamed when something went wrong. The Duruma believed that the ancestors came at night asking for food, clothes and other offerings. It was thought that sometimes an ancestor was not satisfied with the family's offerings and so returned in a white sheet to take them to the spirit world. They were terrified. They took a branch of a thorn tree and beat his grave crying, 'Ah, Shade! We are tired of you. Don't come again!'

Protection against evil powers was sought from the

'medicine man' or 'traditional doctor'. He tried to find the cause of each patient's illness or misfortune. Then he prescribed a medicine he considered powerful enough to destroy the evil power that caused the suffering. Sometimes people came to him for protective charms to drive away harmful powers and he was respected for his power to take care of them. As the Embu traditional doctor began his treatment, he took a piece of broken pottery and filled it with water. Into this he dipped some leaves and shook them to sprinkle the water. Then he pointed to the sun, the great mountain and the sky saying, 'God help me.' He acknowledged his dependence upon the supreme God for his special powers and the water sprinkling symbolized the offences his patient had committed against the community.

Thankfully, many fears and superstitions are now disappearing. But some Africans still feel uneasy about the traditions that continue to grip the older members of their family. Some ask, 'If you don't believe in evil powers, can they harm you?' Most people turn to the local hospital for medical help and care, but traditional doctors are still respected in many villages. They usually spent time listening to their patients' problems which medical doctors today often fail to do. Although their methods were unhygenic and often caused more infection, some of their herbal remedies had great therapeutic value. Although, as in all societies, there were unscrupulous doctors who charged high fees and exploited poor people, many of them really cared for the well-being of the whole community.

Forgiveness

If bitterness or grudges caused a man or woman to curse another and so bring ill health or misfortune, it followed that forgiveness was essential to everyone's well-being. In the Duruma family when a child had done something wrong, he had to come to his father and confess. His father carefully explained why the offence was wrong. Then he took half a mouthful of water and sprayed it over the child, as a sign that he was forgiven. Similarly, when a daughter was preparing for marriage, her parents sat down with her and they recalled all the times they had hurt or offended one another. Then the father again took half a mouthful of water and sprayed it over her, and she knew that there was no more bitterness between them as she began her new life.

Many past traditions recognized the value of 'wholeness' which Christians stress. The needs of body, mind and spirit cannot be separated. Physical suffering is often caused by anxiety, broken relationships and hurt feelings. Healing, therefore, is only effective when peace of mind and spirit has been restored, or when reconciliation has taken place. This is at the heart of the Christian faith. 'God was in Christ reconciling the world to himself.' Those who are at one with God are given grace to forgive and be at peace with one another.

The Old and the New

Jesus, speaking to a Jewish audience, said that a disciple is like a householder who stores in his cupboard 'treasures old and new'. God's laws in the Old Testament were not to be discarded. To most African Christians the customs and beliefs of their people are still precious. They are solid and their roots are deep. Jesus came not to destroy but to fulfil the ways and thought of his own people. In the same way he can fulfil all that is good and true in African tradition. Africans today are proud of their rich heritage and want peoples of other countries to respect and share their special insights and experience. In Kenya, Christians are exploring truly African ways to express their faith, so that they can share with the world their own Christian experience rooted in their own culture.

Jesus also said that the 'new wine' of the kingdom of God could not be contained in 'old wineskins'; the wine would ferment and burst the skins. This is equally true. The kingdom of God is for *all* people of every culture. It does not depend upon, and cannot be confined within, the heritage of any one race. Christians are part of a greater world-wide community and, whoever we are, Christ calls us to make a new beginning.

Praise and Thanksgiving

Praise

O come let us give praise to our God;
let us come before the Lord our Creator.
Lord, the works of your hands are wonderful,
and you continue to make this world more beautiful.
We praise you and worship you, O Lord.

Our land which is full of beauty is yours:
your glory is in the miracle of dawn,
in the beginning of a new day;
it is in the wonder of sun
filtering through the mist.
It is a joy to be alive in your presence.
We praise you and worship you, O Lord.

We see your glory in snow-covered peaks
between mountains,
in moving still waters,
deep down in valleys,
between rocks
everywhere.
We praise you and worship you, O Lord.

Your glory is in the tall palms,
the sandy beaches
and the coral reef;
it is in the shade of a tree on a hot day
and in plantations and crops
that give us food and money.
We praise you and worship you, O Lord.

You loved the world so much
that you came down to us
and became a human being,
to make yourself known to us
and to lay down your life for us.
We praise you and worship you, O Lord.

You created everything in the universe;
you gave life to every plant and animal,
and you created me in your own image;
you gave me my mind and personality,
and the longing
to find your presence in my life.
We praise you and worship you, O Lord.

I will always praise you for your goodness;
I will give thanks and worship;
I will grow in your love.
Help me to reflect your goodness in my life;
to serve you all my days.
There is no other way to praise you,
than to do good
and to show love to my neighbour.
We praise you and worship you, O Lord.

Wonders of Creation

Praise God,
for the mysteries of the universe:
for the wonders of the sky on a clear night;
for stars we cannot count
and the distance between them,
which is more than we can imagine.

Praise him,
for the beauty that surrounds us on earth;
for big oceans and tiny streams,
rivers that run endlessly
and deep blue seas.

Praise him for lakes,
for the rains which fill them
and mountains surrounding them;
for the grandeur of escarpments
and endless plains.

Praise be to God
for his creation of all living things,
for filling the seas and lakes with fish
and giving colour and song to birds;
for filling our world with interest and fascination.

Praise him,
for insects, worms and microscopic creatures;
for bacteria and fungi;
for the delicate balance of nature
and the dependence of one species upon another.

The Wonder of Life

Lord, we do not have to look far
to see the wonders of your creation.
We only have to look at ourselves,
at the mechanisms of the human body.

We praise you for the functions
of parts we cannot see,
which operate without our knowledge.
We praise you for the heart,
like a motor,
pumping blood and oxygen
around the body.

We praise you for the brain,
for mysterious chemical reactions
within our bodies;
for the respiratory system;
for the nucleus within the cell,
and for the complexity of the nucleus.

We praise you for our place in your creation;
for your careful design of body, mind and spirit;
for the challenge of life
and the purpose of our lives together.

We praise you for your wonderful care
and your tireless watch over mankind.
We are happy to praise you;
for you have shown mercy and kindness.
You do not discriminate:
You love us all.

Resources for Living

We give praise for new discoveries each day,
through which we see
your power and majesty.

We praise you for sources of energy
which you provide for our homes
and for industry.
We praise you for gas and electricity
and for our discovery of nuclear power.

We praise you for the discovery of radiation
which enables us to diagnose
and fight disease;
for our knowledge of medicine and drugs
and new ways of helping those who are mentally ill.

Thank you for microscopes
through which we can see
the smallest forms of life,
and through which we learn more
about the different kinds of virus
that cause disease.

We praise you for the smallest units:
for atoms and molecules,
for the bonding of atoms
and the formation of compounds;
for gases, liquids and solids.

Father, the resources of the earth are yours.
They were there from the beginning
for us to find
and use
for the good of all people
for generations to come.
All praise and glory are yours
for ever and ever.
Amen.

Thank You

Thank you Lord for the gift of life:
a healthy body,
strength to do my work,
sight and hearing,
the sense of smell
and the enjoyment of food.
Thank you for eyes to see the wonders of your creation;
for ears to hear sounds of wind and bird song
and the conversation of my friends.
Thank you for legs to walk;
hands to write;
brains to think
and make decisions.

Thank you for rain and sun,
for running water,
for crops of fruit and green vegetables;
for cattle, sheep and goats.
Thank you for the warmth of sunshine on my body.

Thank you for music and dance,
pop stars and new rhythms.
Thank you for the traditional music of our people.

Thank you for this new day;
its opportunity of worship and prayer.

Thank you for houses and good buildings,
hospitals and health centres;
for cars and buses
and the tarmac road.
Thank you for engineers
who design dams and bridges;
whose inventions link together
countries and continents.
Thank you for communications across the world;
for aircraft,

ships,
telephones
and radio,
and for all the discoveries of modern technology.

Thank you for truth
and freedom to worship;
for the freedom to make my own moral decisions.
Thank you that I can say this prayer.

Thank you for joys and happiness
and for the sorrows through which I know
your comfort.

Thank you most of all for sending your Son Jesus Christ:
for his death and resurrection
and for the forgiveness he has made possible for us.
Thank you, Lord.

Thanksgiving for Family Life

Lord, we give thanks
for our cultural heritage,
which helps us,
through the changes of modern life,
to maintain happiness
and close family ties.

We give thanks for all that we have learnt
from our grandparents
of our traditions and folk lore
and for their faith and goodness.

We give thanks
for the feeling of being loved;
for the experience of being cared for;
for the confidence in daily life
that springs from such happiness.

We give thanks
for the value of a new-born child;
for our brothers and sisters;
for the sharing of tasks;
for giving our parents love and strength,
for their wisdom
and for the benefit of their experience.

We give thanks
for your help in our daily activities:
in planting and harvesting;
for your presence in our family prayers,
and for the fellowship of those who visit us.

Thanksgiving for the Church

Father, we give thanks for the church,
your body on earth;
for the fellowship of those who believe,
with whom we have learnt to understand
your Word,
and to feel your presence;
by whom our faith is strengthened,
and with whom we have so much to share.

We thank you for those
whose example and faith
help us in our growth as Christians;
for those who spare time
to answer our questions
and give us encouragement.

We thank you for our church buildings
and every opportunity to worship you
in fellowship with others.
We give thanks for the grace we receive,
as we share your broken body.
We praise you and worship you,
who made us part of that body
for which you gave your life.
Amen.

Thanksgiving for Education

Lord, we thank you for this school
and for every opportunity
to widen our experience of life
and our knowledge of the world;
for friendships
and the guidance of teachers and prefects;
for the benefits we have received this week.

Thank you for strength to work,
for the fitness of my body,
for learning to take care of myself.
Thank you for problems that make me think;
for questions that challenge me,
and for the difficulties I am learning to face.

Thank you for help as I prepare for examinations
and for the work I shall do in my community.
Thank you that I am able to associate with others;
for the enjoyment of talking the whole day
with my fellow students;
for the excitement of going home at the end of term.

Thank you for co-operation
between students and teachers,
between prefects and juniors;
for the help of our Board of Governors
and their wise management of the school.
Thank you for all who guide our lives in the wider
    community.

May we express our thankfulness
as we use our education
to serve you and all mankind.
Amen.

'Thank you that I was given a place in Form 1.
When I was in primary school
I hardly dared hope
that I would do well enough
to come here.
Thank you for helping my parents
to get the money to pay my fees.'

Repentance

Confession

Lord, you see my sins more clearly
than I can myself;
you know when I am untruthful
and when I think evil of others.
You see my anger
and unfairness to my friends.
You know how hard it is for me to forgive.

Lord, you know
when I am indifferent
to your Word, the Bible;
how often I forget
to pray;
the times I come unwillingly
to worship;
and yet I turn to you,
when I am in trouble.

Lord, I have sinned,
without considering how much
you love me.

Forgive me and make me clean,
so that I can obey your call
to take up your cross
and follow you.
Amen.

Confession: Our Thoughts and Actions

Lord, when we come to you,
your love shows up our imperfections
and we are ashamed.
Lord, take control of our lives
and direct our thoughts and actions.

Forgive us when our feelings control our behaviour;
for giving way to anger, jealousy and bitterness;
for unhealthy thoughts
which hinder our studies
and our relationship with you.
Lord, take control of our lives
and direct our thoughts and actions.

Forgive our addiction to bad habits;
our bad language;
our misuse of your name
and the lies we tell each other.
Lord, take control of our lives
and direct our thoughts and actions.

We are ashamed of
our conversations with one another,
and our lack of respect
in all our relationships.
Forgive us.
Lord, take control of our lives
and direct our thoughts and actions.

Forgive us: we have been careless
with other people's property;
we have been reckless
and irresponsible.
Lord, take control of our lives
and direct our thoughts and actions.

Lord, you have given us our homes
and families to provide and care for us.
Forgive our disobedience
and lack of respect of our elders.
*Lord, take control of our lives
and direct our thoughts and actions.*
Amen.

Confession: Our Relationships in School

Lord, our school could be a happier place
than we have made it.
We are ashamed of the things we do
and the way we speak.
We take our school for granted
and we complain about so many things.
We ignore our friends
and abuse them behind their backs;
we tell tales
and say nasty things about others;
we bully those younger than ourselves
and insult our classmates . . .
Forgive us.

Lord, you have given to us
the opportunity to learn
and prepare ourselves for the future;
but we have wasted much of our time
and have not respected or considered
those who want to work.
We have made so much noise
that others have found it hard to concentrate.
We have missed lessons
or been late to class
and have deceived our teachers
with weak excuses.
We have ignored the rules laid down for us
and have held grudges against prefects and teachers.
Forgive us.

Forgive our pride
in thinking others less capable
than ourselves.
Forgive our jealousy
when others do what is right.
Lord, you have set us an example

of how to treat others:
but we have deliberately started arguments
and insulted one another.
When we are in the wrong,
we do not bother to apologize.
We have destroyed friendships between others
in order to gain friends for ourselves.
Forgive us.

Forgive us for doing to others
what we would not like done to ourselves.
Forgive us for joining in with others;
in laughing at and victimizing
another student.
Lord, take away from us the love of sinning,
and give us the will and grace
to follow you.
Amen.

Confession: Our Evasions

Father of us all,
we confess
we are careless and indifferent;
we are afraid to stand up for the right,
or to protest against the wrong;
we follow our own selfish ends.
Forgive us.

We have been so absorbed in our own interests
that we have not noticed
when other students have been tired and lonely;
we have ignored signs
of strain and tiredness
in our closest friends,
and have done nothing to help.
Forgive us.

At home we have been asked to help,
when our parents were tired or busy,
and we have been awkward and selfish.
In so many situations,
people have asked for a little of our time
and we have deliberately found other things to do.
Forgive us.

Help us to see ourselves as you see us;
to see the weakness of our excuses
and to know when our actions
are mean and selfish.
Amen.

Beyond Ourselves

Your Kingdom Come

Father, may your kingdom come;
may your will be done
on earth as it is in heaven.

Father, we give thanks
that your kingdom is here in our midst;
that your kingdom is present
in those who have repented
and changed their ways
to follow Jesus,
and who, in faith,
have accepted Jesus Christ
as their personal Saviour.

We pray that your kingdom may grow;
that those who have turned away from you
through some difficult experience,
may turn again
and have faith to believe
that you are there,
everyday,
in work
and in rest.

Father, may your kingdom come in our society.
May your will be done in courts of justice,
in the governments of the world,
in business
and among all who are responsible for employment.

Where there is oppression,
may your kingdom come.
Liberate those who are victims of racial discrimination,
that they may enjoy the peace
they have been denied.

May your kingdom come in the lives
of judges,
magistrates
and civil servants.
May those who lead us
become true servants of the kingdom
and of your community.

May your kingdom come in our land,
in better living conditions for slum dwellers
and beggars;
that they may be rehabilitated in homes
and schools.

May your kingdom come
in our family relationships,
as parents and children come to understand
and show concern for one another.

May your kingdom come in us
as we learn to do the difficult things
our Lord taught us;
as we settle quarrels
and learn to think more of others
than we do of ourselves.

And . . .
May we be ready
at the final coming of your kingdom . . .
In the name of Jesus Christ our Lord.
Amen.

Some Family Problems

66 My family is divided; there is no unity. 99

66 My parents are so poor, I don't know whether I will finish my education. 99

66 My mother is dead. 99

66 My father has taken another wife. 99

66 My parents have been killed. 99

66 My father is always drunk; there is no love between the members of my family. 99

66 My father is so harsh; I can't ask him anything. 99

Lord, may we remember
the family is the basic human community
which you created.
Help us to do all we can
to maintain good relationships,
unity and happiness,
to make our families
communities of love
and service.

We pray for those who suffer
as a result of broken homes
and misunderstandings within the family;
for those who lack the love and support
of parents;
for those who have lost parents;
for families dying of hunger;
for orphans and destitute children.

Lord, help us to see beyond personal difficulties
to the problems of other families;
that from our own experience of sorrow,
we may share the sufferings
and loneliness of others,
and be able to give them
love and understanding.
Amen.

Family Life

Lord, we pray for our families,
for peace and unity;
for self-control between husband and wife;
for responsibility and self-reliance.
We pray that parents may be firm and reasonable;
that they may understand us
and that we may understand them.
Teach us daily to forgive one another
and to come together in times of need.

Lord, you know the difficulties
facing each of our families:
help our parents,
our brothers and sisters,
wherever they are,
and in whatever they do.

Lord, keep my family safe
and free from evil
while I am away at school.
And save me from the sorrow
of hearing bad news from home.

Help me to respect each member of my family
and be thankful
for all my family has done for me.
In the name of Jesus Christ, our Lord.
Amen.

'Sometimes I'm exasperated
with my whole family
because something's gone wrong.
Give me patience and understanding.'

For World Peace

Father, we pray for the peoples of the world;
for peace and unity
and for the brotherhood of man.
We pray for those oppressed by selfish rulers;
for those harassed by dictatorship;
for countries under colonial rule;
for those who suffer at the hands of terrorists
and hijackers.

We pray for peace in the countries of . . .
where there is violence and bloodshed.
We pray for a new stability in their political affairs;
for an end to executions
and the massacre of innocent people;
for economic progress,
and for freedom to enjoy peace.

We pray for a new understanding
in discussions between world leaders
and among ordinary people.

We pray for world disarmament:
that the money spent on weapons of war
may be used to feed the hungry.
May we too, recognize other people
as our brothers and sisters
and so bring peace.
Amen.

For Liberation

Father, we pray for respect and equality
between all peoples;
for an end to racial discrimination,
prejudice and hatred,
violence and bloodshed,
political and religious strife.
Let freedom be for all mankind,
regardless of colour, race or creed.
Let all peoples see
that each man, woman and child
has a right
to justice,
education
and life.

Lord, guide leaders of liberation movements,
that they may gain justice for their people
without violence.
Take away all bitterness.
Give to the oppressed
strength to bear pain
and grace to forgive.
Amen.

For Development

Lord, we give you thanks
for the benefits of development:
for better means of communication;
for education;
for better health facilities;
for industry and cars;
for new methods of agriculture
and new machinery for cultivation;
for the gift of nuclear power . . .
But we are concerned, Lord,
that we may use your gifts more responsibly:
guide our people's decisions
that we may have industrial progress
without pollution.

Teach us to plan
for the welfare of future generations:
when we cut down trees
for our own benefit,
remind us to plant more
for tomorrow's world.

Help us to seek
more responsible and just ways
of sharing the earth's fuel resources.

Teach those you have entrusted
with the use of nuclear power
to use it in industry
with the utmost care,
for the benefit
and peace of mankind . . .
and not to destroy every living thing
nor leave the world uninhabited.
Amen.

For the Very Poor

Lord, we are concerned
for refugees;
for all whose homes have been wrecked
by floods and earthquakes.

We pray for people
so poor
that they cannot help themselves;
whose subsistence crops
have been destroyed by climatic disasters;
for people who live in areas
where rainfall is unreliable
and varies from year to year.
We pray for small children
who die of malnutrition,
and others who suffer from disease
because their mothers do not understand
the values of different kinds of foods.

We pray for little children,
too young
to pray for themselves.

For the Unemployed

Father, we are concerned,
for millions unemployed:
for those whose ambitions are frustrated
because they cannot find a job.
Give them courage to persist
without becoming involved in crime.

Father, we are concerned
for those who avoid responsibility
and do not appreciate
the dignity of work.
We pray for beggars and parking boys,
for prostitutes and thieves,
for those who see no hope,
no future.

May the employed members of our community
learn to share the opportunity to work
with others;
that they may not hold too many posts
while many are jobless.

And for Others . . .

We pray for old people
who have no one to care for them;
for those ill in hospital
or who have become sick
through fear and anxiety.

We pray for men and women in prison:
help all whose minds and intentions
are evil;
give them a concern
for the progress of our people.

Father, we are concerned
for those whose homes
have been invaded by thieves;
for helpless victims
of violence.

Lord, we are concerned
for the physically handicapped;
for the blind, the dumb and the lame.
We are concerned for the mentally ill,
for those who do not have the ability
to learn and think clearly,
or who have deep personal problems.
They are part of our community;
they are one with us . . .
Help us to care for them,
to help them find a place in society
and to know that they are loved
and wanted.
Amen.

For the Right Use of Money

Lord, help us to resist the temptation
which money presents.

Help those with financial problems and debts
to avoid dishonest and corrupt ways.

Help us all not to be influenced
by the materialistic standards
of other countries.
Help us not to envy
those who are better off than ourselves.
Help us to close the gap
between rich and poor
in our own country.

Guide all managers and directors
of large business concerns,
that they may have steadiness of purpose
and do what is lawful and right.

Strengthen our faith and courage
to face evil and corruption.
Amen.

For the Church

Lord, the church isn't just a building:
the church is people,
and we are part of it.
Yet, Lord, we are not always
serious about our faith.

We pray for all church leaders and ministers,
that they may have spiritual insight and integrity,
strength and wisdom;
that they may set a good example
and understand the needs
of younger Christians.
Help preachers to communicate
their faith
and to make it relevant
to the needs of all.

Give harmony:
may the old be open to change,
and the young learn to be patient.

Bless all evangelists
who are taking the Christian faith
to new areas.
Strengthen smaller churches,
where work is often frustrated
by lack of money.

Lord, many people come to our churches
and do not find a welcome,
or an answer to their questions;
they come in spiritual hunger
and are not satisfied;
they come, longing for acceptance,
seeking a new security
and a feeling of being loved.
Make us a welcoming

and loving fellowship
that no one will turn away
unsatisfied.
Amen.

For Christian Unity

May the church
join people together throughout the world.
May there be peace and unity
between all Christian denominations.
Heal our divisions.

We pray for the church in Ireland
that a new understanding
and a closer relationship
may grow between Catholics and Protestants.

Cleanse your church
of corruption and hypocrisy,
hatred and prejudice,
that we may live as one body.

For the Persecuted

We pray for Christians who are denied freedom
to worship
and who suffer for the truth;
for those wrongly condemned in prison –
in Ethiopia,
Poland,
Russia
and Romania.
Strengthen their faith;
vindicate them
and give them the victory and peace
that overcomes undeserved suffering.

Teach us also to stand for what we believe
and make us ready to suffer for your sake.
Amen.

For School Life

Lord, be with us in this school:
help us in our studies,
and give us confidence to face problems.
Help us to pay attention in class,
even when the work is difficult and boring.

Teach us to accept failure
as well as success.
Remind us that education
is more than acquiring certificates:
it is for life,
to enable us to live with others
and to create good relationships.
Give us wisdom
and insight into one another's problems.

Help us not to follow the crowd
but to think and act
independently and responsibly.

Help us in sport and games
to keep the rules
and to be fair and generous.

Help us when we are too proud
to say 'sorry' to our friends.

Help those who are studying hard
to achieve their ambition.
Help us to respect
all who come into our school
and who work in it.

May we use our education to make . . .
a great and strong nation;
to serve our people in business,
in medicine and in education;
and make us able to communicate with
and serve peoples of other races and cultures.

Help students with fees' problems
and those who have had to return home
because of sickness.
Help them to overcome their hardships soon,
so that they can rejoin the school
and continue learning.

Within
Ourselves

Love

❝Love's meaning is life's secret.**❞**

Jesus said, **❝**Love one another.**❞**

Lord, I find it hard to love
without taking revenge.
Teach me that to accept defeat
is greater than revenge;
it keeps one's mind at rest
and clear of guilt.
Help me to use my hands to express love
rather than hatred
and to remember
that hate and love cannot grow together.

Lord, I find it hard to love
without finding fault,
without prejudice
and discrimination.
Lord, give me love like yours
that is not 'choosy',
that transcends
my love for family and friends
and is patient and kind.

Lord, give me a clear vision
of your love,
when I meet it
in the face of a stranger,
in the poor
and in the unwanted.

Help me to love unselfishly
and to remember that love demands sacrifice
of time and energy.

Love works willingly
and is not reluctant or grudging.
It does not seek the admiration and praise of others.
Love grows within
through prayer
and through reliance upon your Holy Spirit.
Love gives new life
progress and fulfilment.

Lord, help me to love others
as you have loved me,
in giving your Son
for my forgiveness.
Amen.

Peace

Lord, we pray for peace among ourselves,
as well as for peace among nations;
for in peace, we find happiness
and can live as your children.
Teach us to trust one another,
so that we can share our problems,
joys and sorrows,
and communicate with each other without fear.
Help us to trust you more and more
that we may have the quiet confidence
which leads to understanding relationships with others.

Tolerance

❝ God, there's this girl I just can't stand;
and there's this teacher who constantly
gets on my nerves! **❞**

Lord, you have created me in your image;
you have called me by my name
and I am yours;
you have made me unique.
Help me now to accept the uniqueness
in others
and so continue your creative work.
Give me grace to accept their 'otherness'
and their shortcomings,
because, like them,
I am imperfect.

Help me to understand all those
I live with in school
and at home,
so that I do not hurt their feelings
by doing or saying the wrong thing.
Lord, give me humility
to recognize
that through you
I can learn to accept other people
as they are.

Lord,
help me to respect people of other religions,
ideologies,
and cultures.
Help me to remember that my opinions
are not necessarily the best
and that if I listen to others
I will learn from them.

Learning to Forgive

It's very hard, Lord,
to obey your command to forgive.
I am angry with my friends
when they let me down;
when they despise me,
mock me,
or criticize me.
It's hard to accept their apology.
Sometimes I even dare to think
the other person
doesn't deserve to be forgiven.
And yet I know
that to hold ill feelings and hatred
within my heart
is a heavy burden.
Help me, Father, to forgive completely,
and not with an unspoken grudge.
Give me the grace to forgive
and the will to forget.
Give me the wisdom to understand
that in forgiving and forgetting,
I may help to build a better community
and can dare to come to you
for the forgiveness of my sins.
Amen.

Learning to Give

Lord, you have commanded us
to offer hospitality
and to give ungrudgingly.

But am I a giver?
Lord, it is hard to give to people
who irritate you;
I give things to friends
to gain favour;
I give things
I will never need again,
and I rarely give to those
who cannot afford to reciprocate.
Often I give
for people
to see how much I am giving,
and when no one thanks me,
I am offended.

Lord, transform my attitude.
Help me to give,
not because I am afraid of being called mean,
but because I want to give.
Teach me to share with others
whatever little I possess.

Help me to give
according to my gifts and skills,
so that I can help my classmates,
instead of fearing
that they will get higher marks.

Give me wisdom
to recognize genuine need
in beggars
and those who come to me for help,
and teach me how to help them best.

My Struggle with Faith

I fled from him,
but he came after me,
beckoning to me,
calling me to come to him
for rest.
In love he searched for me,
sorrowing over my folly,
sorrowing over my stubborn mind.
I refused to believe
that he was born,
that he was crucified for my sake;
that for me, he was,
in humble silence,
reduced to a suffering servant.
Yes, God came to me in Jesus;
in a man of flesh,
combining all love and goodness,
all strength and gentleness . . .
He whom all tongues confess as Lord.

He comes to you;
he bids you
to come to him,
for rest,
for forgiveness,
for life.
Won't you come?

Doubts and Faith

Lord, we are confused
by much we learn in school.
There are so many mysteries in nature
beyond our comprehension,
and sometimes we doubt your existence.

Science makes us doubt:
we want to believe in you,
but we have no physical evidence
that you created the universe
and it is hard to believe
what we cannot see.

The first disciples
did not find it easy to believe.
Help us, like them, to be honest
and help each other
in our discussions.

Let us never close our minds.
Make our thinking more positive,
that we may build our faith
upon the good things we have discovered.

May your Holy Spirit make us more aware
of your presence,
in all we do
in class, in sport,
and bring us closer to you,
day by day.

Lord, give us faith:
convince us of your reality.
May your Holy Spirit work in us
and strengthen our growing faith.
Help us to understand with our minds
what we feel in our hearts.
Amen.

Our Lack of Trust

Lord, we believe in you,
yet we fail to trust you completely.
We find it hard to see your guidance
in our lives.

We find it hard,
when someone close to us dies,
or when we are sick,
to go on trusting you.
We turn to you
and blame you.
We feel helpless
and wonder whether you really care.
Sometimes it seems
our prayers are not answered.

Help us not to despair,
but to go on believing in your presence,
even when everything seems to go against us.
Help us to be strong
in times of weakness;
and help us when things go well
not to forget you.
Give us faith
that will not fail us
in trouble and in danger.

Lord, we are confused
when we see your church divided.
We lose faith,
because often Christian fellowship activities
are boring,
or strained,
or reduced to a minimum.

We long for a deeper fellowship
with one another,
to share our inspiration.

Lord, help us to develop
a more mature faith
and to understand you more,
so that we can go on believing,
whatever our circumstances.

Responsibility

Lord, you made us to care
for one another,
for younger children,
for animals,
for neighbours,
for the poor
and for our environment.
But we confess that we have neglected
or misused our responsibility
and have brought suffering or inconvenience
to others.
In fear of shame,
we have denied that we were responsible.
Forgive us.

Help us to work for the benefit of others:
to fulfil our duties
with punctuality and care,
without grumbling,
remembering the needs and circumstances
of those we serve.

Help us to face up to responsibilities
of citizenship,
and family life.
Restrain and make us more careful
in our use of the earth's dwindling resources.
Let us not spoil your creation
by the litter we leave around.

Make us more responsible
in loyalty to the church,
in worship
and in witness.

Our Personal Freedom

Lord, you created us and made us free,
and we value that freedom
above all else:
freedom within,
to think and choose,
to express ideas
and to worship you without fear.

Help us to use freedom
in ways which will not harm
or limit the freedom of others.

Lord, you understand our need,
as teenagers,
to be free.
Help those who are frustrated
by over-possessive and strict parents;
and give to us your grace
that we may act in such a way
that our parents will trust us . . .
and may we not abuse that trust.

Give wisdom to
those who will soon leave school:
that they will not misuse their new freedom.

Deliver us from compromise:
make us free
to stand up for what is right.

Lord, show us more clearly
the truth that sets us free.
Liberate us from our sins
and bad habits;
and use us to bring freedom to others.
Amen.

Our Future

Lord, when I think about the future,
I begin to worry.

In exams help me to remember what I have learnt
and to understand the questions correctly.
Give me confidence,
a fresh, cool and relaxed mind
and wisdom to apply my knowledge.
Lord, hear our prayer.
Our future belongs to you.

Lord, the future stretches before me
like a long dark tunnel,
leading into the unknown.
After my exams,
will I get to university?
Or will I begin the endless search
for a job?
Will I make enough money?

Lord, my future is in your hands.
Help me to look honestly
at my own ability
and to know if I have the right skills
for the jobs that attract me.
Lord, hear our prayer.
Our future belongs to you.

Help me to choose a career
in which I can work honestly,
and avoid corruption and immorality.
Help me to choose a career
that will not hinder
my future responsibility to my family
or destroy their happiness.

Lord, I would like to be rich
and have everything I need.
Yet I fear I will forget you
and that there is life after death.
Help me to choose a career
that will bring true happiness,
satisfaction and fulfilment;
in which I can serve my people
and not forget to help the needy members
of our community.
Lord, hear our prayer.
Our future belongs to you.

Lord, I would like to be independent
and never to have to rely
on the charity of others.
But help me to face the possibility
of unemployment
if that is my future.
If I fail,
give me courage to begin again.
Lord, hear our prayer.
Our future is in your hands.

Lord, I have great hopes
of a bright future;
a good job
and a happy marriage.
Help me to find a partner
who shares my interests,
so that our life together
may be fully satisfying.
Lord, hear our prayer.
Our future is in your hands.

Our Need of Help

Lord, when we are in trouble
there is no one really able to help
but you.
You know before we pray
what is worrying us.
Help us not to forget your presence,
and when we begin to doubt,
strengthen our faith.

Help us not to waste time,
or form bad habits,
or to be influenced
by popular opinion.
Help us to think for ourselves,
to decide independently
what is right,
and to believe what is good.

Help us to be truthful,
to own up
when we are at fault
and to accept correction.
Take away our pride.

Help us to give praise and encouragement
to others,
rather than criticism.

May we be slow to anger,
careful in speech,
and eager to help.
When problems arise enable us
to tackle them with confidence.

Lord, we find it hard to reflect your love
when people offend us.
Help us to forgive
and not to take revenge.

Help us to persevere when life is difficult,
to understand our weaknesses and mistakes
and to know that we cannot always have
everything we want.

Lord, each day is full of temptations
from sunrise to sunset.
Take all evil thoughts from our minds,
so that we harm no one
and can serve you always.

Lord, I am happy
when I hear your name praised.
Your great power helps me to survive
all my problems.
I hope always to receive your strength.
Amen.

Following Jesus: A Prayer for Confirmation

Lord Jesus,
we have decided to follow you,
not because we have been forced to come,
but because we want to.
Lord Jesus,
this is our decision.

We know that your way
means real commitment,
sacrifice,
carrying your cross,
giving time to help others.
Lord, help us to follow you completely.

For what better friend can we have?
Who else can we trust so wholeheartedly?
You are the Way, the Truth and the Life,
through whom we see God.
You have loved us freely.
Help us to follow joyfully in your footsteps.

Transform our lives;
let your teachings and parables
guide our actions and speech.
Help us to obey your great commandment
to love one another.

Thank you for the Bible:
help me to be regular in my study of your Word,
and to obey its commands in my life.
Teach me to pray
and find peace in your presence.

Help me to think less of self
and more of others.
Give me your grace and generosity
to spend time
to help those who are handicapped,
disabled or sick.
Help me to choose a career
in which I can serve my community.

Lord,
the world makes it tough
for me to follow you;
give me strength to resist temptation,
courage to stand up for what is right,
and strength of will never to turn back.
May I discover the true happiness
that comes from following
and trusting you,
always.
Amen.

The Christian
Year

Christmas in Kenya

Christmas is a time to share happiness;
to give presents,
to laugh and joke together;
to thank God for everything.

Christmas in Kenya is a time of sunshine,
blue skies,
flowers,
shady trees
and the song of birds,
while other parts of the world are cold
and wrapped in snow.

Thank you, Father,
for all the joy and happiness of Christmas:
for the new clothes and shoes that are bought for us;
for the goats and cocks we slaughter;
for the food and gifts we receive;
for the love and generosity of our parents and friends;
for the example of the wise men
who first brought gifts to you.

We rejoice this Christmas:
for our Saviour comes
to bring us joy.
May the song of the Christ Child
be sung in our land
upon the mountains,
down in the valleys
and across the plains,
in every house
and in every compound.

We rejoice with Christians all over the world.
We rejoice with children of other lands:
children of many colours
and ways of life.
May the peace and blessings of the Christ Child
be for all children;
May we grow in the way of Jesus;
and know the real meaning of Christmas.

The Meaning of Christmas

Christmas is the coming together
of families,
relatives
and friends,
to show love for one another
in giving and in song;
to rejoice together
that the Son of God is born,
a child.

Help us, Lord,
in our feasting and merriment,
to remember
that Christmas is people:
the family of Mary and Joseph
and a new baby.

Help us to remember the simplicity
of the first Christmas:
the sign of a child
born in a stable
to die for us.

The child's body born at Bethlehem
was broken
for our forgiveness.
Give us grace this Christmas
as we share his body;
and may we give you honour and worship.

In glory you were rich,
but you came down:
you were born into a poor family
because you loved us.

Thank you, Lord, for all the kindness
in the hearts of people at Christmas,
moved to give,
to the underprivileged,
the poor,
the weak
and the disabled . . .
for gifts given to those who cannot afford them.

Bless all new-born children
and be with those who are near to death.

Fill our hearts with your compassion:
help us to be more eager to give
than to receive.
Be born in us
and grow in us . . .
Amen.

Lent: The Suffering of Jesus

Blessed be the name of Jesus,
who died to save us.
Blessed be Jesus,
who had compassion on us.
Blessed be Jesus,
who suffered loneliness,
rejection
and pain,
for our sakes.
Blessed be Jesus,
through whose cross
I am forgiven.
Lord Jesus, deepen my understanding
of your suffering and death.

Lord Jesus,
each day you are hurt again
by my sin
and by my forgetfulness
to carry your cross in my life:
forgive me.
As I look in worship towards your cross,
the symbol of my faith,
help me to share the
carrying of that cross
without complaint.

As you suffered for me,
teach me to suffer
for others
and for all that is true.
Amen.

Easter

Jesus Christ, you are Lord!
We give you honour and worship,
for you died and rose again
and you are at the right hand
of God our Father.
You have overcome death,
that we, through faith in you,
may have eternal life.
We give you honour
that our faith,
and the faith of the whole church today,
is founded on that first Easter Day.

By your resurrection,
you overcame the power of evil;
help us now to overcome
the power of temptation in our lives.
May your love destroy
our selfishness,
our tempers,
our pride
and our doubts;
that we may share
the victory
of your risen life,
and that we may know
the reality
of your living presence
within us.
Amen

Pentecost

We give thanks for the first day of Pentecost:
for the gift of tongues
and the gifts of love, peace
and joy.

May the Holy Spirit come to us
like the wind and fire
as he came to those first disciples.
May he come
as we pray,
and may we feel his power.
May he increase our faith
and change our lives . . .
and may the fruits of the Spirit
be seen in us.
Amen.

Meditations

Fears

We are afraid,
afraid of people,
of the dark,
of evil,
of illness,
of death.
We are afraid of insects that bring disease,
of snakes,
of attack from wild animals,
of accidents.

We fear many things,
but we don't like to admit it to anyone.
We let our friends think we are brave,
but deep down we are afraid.

We are afraid of being scorned
and laughed at by other students,
of being despised for doing right.

We fear the future;
leaving school to begin work,
to take responsibility.
We fear the final exams,
failure,
the prospect of unemployment
and poverty.

We are afraid of being sent home
with a bad report at the end of term;
afraid of being sent to the head
for some misdeed.
We are afraid of punishment,
of suspension,
of being sent home from school.

We are afraid of answering a question in class;
afraid of looking foolish before others.

We are afraid of fire.
We are scared at the slightest sound
we hear in the night,
afraid that thieves may break in
and attack us.

We are afraid of the fate
that may face us in the course of a day;
that sad news may come in the form of a letter,
or a phone call,
or a visit.

We are afraid when problems face our country
and the world.
We are afraid of war,
of tribal conflicts,
of those nations who have atomic weapons,
of flood and earthquake;
of anything which might destroy our homes
and bring death to innocent people.

'I am afraid to accept Jesus Christ,
and to join Christian meetings;
I am afraid that people
will start watching me
and asking questions.
I fear hypocrisy and fanaticism
among Christian students.
I fear the second coming of our Lord;
I fear his judgement.'

Our Fear of Death

Lord, we are afraid that death
will come suddenly,
depriving us of the good things
we hope for in the future,
preventing us from fulfilling our ambitions.

We fear
that death can take away
our close friends,
our brothers, sisters and parents.
Death separates us,
leaves us unhappy,
helpless and lonely.
As we see the body laid in a coffin
and buried,
there is so little we can do;
we can only stand
and watch.

Fear of Evil Powers

We fear evil spirits:
we fear them although most of us
do not believe they exist.
We fear to walk out after dark,
because our parents tell us
that evil spirits are about.
We fear the spirits of our ancestors,
whose needs were not fulfilled by our parents,
or by ourselves.
We fear that they will come to us
during the nights
to demand their needs.
We are afraid that if we worship God,
our ancestors will harm us.
We fear bad dreams
and torment after death.
We fear going to the graves of our relatives,
whose spirits have power to do evil.
We fear going to the sacred places
where our people pray.
We fear our elders,
because they do not understand our problems.
We fear the power of evil
in witchcraft and wizards.
We fear to quarrel with old men
and old women
who can curse us
when we offend them.
We fear to dishonour our parents,
to bring hatred to the family,
to be cursed in anger.

Lord, fill us with your peace,
and give us faith to overcome all fear.

The Presence of God

God is not far away;
he is not out of reach.
He, who existed before the universe,
who created
and has power over all things,
is here,
in our worship.
He is not brown or black or white;
he is the Father of all
and through him we live.

As I look up at the sky at night,
I feel he is watching me
and taking care of me.
I find his presence on the mountain;
in the intricate design and colour of flowers;
in tall trees,
and majestic buildings.
I see him in the rain,
in our water supply,
and in the thunder and lightning.
All nature reflects his glory.

I see him in happy, smiling, laughing people;
in the trusting face of a little child.
I hear him calling to me in the needs of others:
in the leper,
the blind man,
the beggar,
stretching out his hands
for help.

He is in the crowd,
the preacher's word,
the sorrowful songs of those who mourn,
the repentant sinner.

He is near in all our experiences,
in sickness and loneliness,
and when we are near to death.
He is with me when I have a problem
and when I pray,
I know that he has been near
to quieten my fears
and to soothe my unhappiness . . .
and I cease to worry about tomorrow.

I feel his presence when I enter a church;
when I am quiet, thinking,
or reading my Bible.

He is near me
when I have to walk along a lonely road
and fear attack from wild animals.

He is with us in all the confusion
of modern life.
He comes to us in Jesus Christ,
to live among us;
to make himself known to us,
yesterday,
today,
and tomorrow.

Jesus

Jesus impressed me,
the way he talked to people:
they stopped whatever they were doing
to listen to him.
And he spoke,
not like a political leader,
wanting to organize and control them,
but as though they were his whole family,
as though he was talking
to his real brothers and sisters,
telling them stories of everyday experiences,
of shepherds and families . . .
Yes, Jesus makes us feel that God cares for us.

When people hurt him,
he never sought revenge;
when he was tired,
and people came to him for help,
he found the strength and time
to talk with them,
and heal them.

He found time for the woman at the well . . .
and she began to think about herself
and her relationships,
as she had never done before,
and her whole life was changed.

He brought
sight to the blind,
strength to the lame,
life to the dead.

Yet he was human like me . . .
tired and hungry,
and hurt by the hardness
and meanness of other people.
God's presence was hard to find
that day on the cross,
when he cried out,
'My God, my God,
why have you forsaken me?'

Jesus, Son of Mary,
I would like to have seen you
performing your miracles;
I would like to have listened
to your words.
Lord Jesus,
I would like to see your power
at work
in people
around me today.

Jesus, Live Within Me

Lord Jesus,
you made yourself a servant.
Yet I am so unwilling to serve,
to treat others as my equals.
If I see a beggar,
I want to walk by
and forget him.
Yet you taught me to treat him
as I would like to be treated myself;
as though I was in his place.

Lord Jesus,
I need you to live within me;
to change my life,
and make me a new person.

Lord Jesus,
you cared for me and suffered for me;
you carried my burden of sin and doubt;
you were crucified upon the cross for my sins.

Jesus, Son of God,
I would like to imitate your ways,
your attitude,
your life:
to spare time for others,
to lessen their suffering,
and to forgive.

Lord,
teach me to behave to others
in my village or town streets,
as you did in the streets of Galilee.

Suffering

Suffering is the experience of all peoples.
It is poverty,
having no money to help yourself.
It is hunger, famine, drought and disease, death . . .
having nobody to help you.
Suffering is unemployment:
losing your dignity
as a person in the community.
It is failure:
feeling that life is not worth living . . .
that everyone is against you.
Suffering is to be the victim
of violence,
persecution and oppression.

Suffering is a consequence of development:
when a friend dies in a plane crash;
when an accident occurs in a factory;
when a car overturns.

I see suffering in a child
left all day and all night
without food,
because his mother is drunk.
I see suffering in a woman
whose husband beats her everyday
and destroys her peace and happiness.
I see suffering in a refugee,
with no home,
no shelter,
no welcome.
I see suffering in the loneliness
of old people
and young people
in the city,

separated
from the security
of family life.

And, Lord, I myself
have caused so much suffering to others,
intentionally and unintentionally,
by my indifference,
selfishness
and impatience.
Forgive me.

When We Suffer

Lord, we are afraid of suffering,
afraid of the unbearable experiences
the future may hold for us.
Sometimes we complain
of small pains and discomforts:
help us to grow up.
Give us patience,
and strength of body, mind and spirit.

If we suffer
help us not to despair.
Increase our faith
and teach us to suffer
in silence.

If there is something you want to teach us
through suffering,
open our eyes and reveal it to us.
Help us not to be bitter
but to see
that in Christ
even the unbearable
brings deeper happiness,
for Christ can take hard experiences
and use them for our good.

Save us from self-pity
and teach us to recognize
and to help those who suffer
more than ourselves.
Use our experience to make us more sensitive
to the needs of others
and teach us real compassion.

May we look at the suffering of Jesus
challenging us
to accept pain,
to carry the cross,
to stand up for what is true
whatever the consequences.

What Is Life?

What is life?
Life is mystery . . . Unfold it!
Life is opportunity . . . Utilize it!
Life is risk . . . Respect it!

What is life?
Life is what you make it.
It is but a dream,
a gamble.
Life is concerned with the business
and pleasures of the world.

Life is short:
we have too little time
to show love and kindness.

Life is a gift:
it is that expanse of time God gives,
that we may learn to live at peace with others
and appreciate all that he created.

What is life?
It is to die:
a boring game that comes to an end.
Life is bitterness and sorrow,
with a touch,
here and there,
of happiness.

Life is good
when you have no problems to face;
enjoyable when your problems
are shared by another.
Life is best
when you have peace within yourself
and with God.

Life is full of ups and downs:
it is a rough journey,
but love eases it along the way.

Life is a struggle,
for reform,
for change,
for a better world . . .

To live is to challenge structures,
old accepted ways,
exploitation . . .

To live is to work;
to face new opportunities,
to accept responsibility.

To live is to care
for people and relationships;
to share sorrow and happiness.

To live is to appreciate your environment:
to be fascinated by the wonder
of flowers and animals and insects;
to respect all people
and to find God.

Life is believing,
trusting,
having faith in Jesus Christ,
through everyday experiences.
'Follow me' he said,
'and you will have abundant life.'

Life is a preparation for death;
it is learning how to die.
Life without hope is meaningless;
life in Christ is everlasting.

Life is God's most precious gift to us . . .
What is life to you?

Happiness: The Good Life

What is happiness?
Happiness is
being successful,
having good health
and no family problems.
Happiness is when things happen
the way you'd like them to happen . . .
to receive good news or a present.
It is going home at the end of term,
meeting again with brothers and sisters,
with parents and friends.

Happiness is the enjoyment of interesting
and amusing books;
listening to records;
watching a film;
sharing our views with others;
eating good food
and the good time we have eating it.

Happiness is to study hard,
to pass exams
and get the right job;
to see the fruits of your work.

It is to live simply,
not to have too much or too little;
but to have the essentials of life . . .
enough food and clothes,
enough money,
enough education,
and prospects for the future.

When you are happy,
there's a smile on your face;
so that wherever you go,
people know you are happy.

Happiness is people:
a man and woman getting married;
understanding between members of your family;
taking presents to your grandmother,
who brought up your parents and cared for them.
It is feeling wanted and loved,
or watching a baby grow up;
being made to feel that you matter.

Happiness is found
in loving your neighbour as yourself,
justice,
self-control,
humility,
forgiveness,
generosity.
True happiness is within:
to have love, peace and faith.

Happiness is to know Jesus Christ:
to experience his presence in our hearts;
to allow him
to transform our relationships,
so that there are no misunderstandings,
conflicts or quarrels.

Happiness is found in service to the community
and brings true development
to the life of our nation.

Yet we find it hard to live the good life
and hold to our values
in modern life.

True happiness cannot be bought or sold;
it is received . . .
God's precious gift
which increases
as we share it with others.

My Vision of a Better World

I would like to see justice, love and peace
for all mankind;
I would like to reduce competition
and hatred between nations.

It would be wonderful
if each man could know the meaning of brotherhood;
if each child had enough milk every day;
if the rich really helped the poor,
and if the poor, in their way, helped the rich;
if there were no more wars,
no more suffering,
no more hatred . . .

Yet, peace and justice and unity for the world
begin
here and now,
with us.
'Do unto others
as you would have them do to you.'
Let us start with the way we treat our families,
our friends
and the passer-by . . .
The world would be a better place,
if we were not so anxious to tell others their mistakes,
while blind to our own faults;
if we could just stop criticizing
and condemning others.

The world will be a better place,
if we respect people for themselves
and not for who and what they are;
if we realize that everyone has a right
to his own opinion;
if we show appreciation for what others do;
if we care not only for those we love,
but also for some we find it hard to love . . .

My ideal world is one in which God's power is seen
and God's presence recognized;
a world in which men and women respond to God
and seek the welfare of mankind.

Personal Prayers from Individual Students

Personal Thanksgiving

'I love and adore my grandmother,
who tells me of our traditions long ago
and of her people's faith in God.
I thank you for letting her live so long
to share these treasures of the past
with my brothers and me.'

'How good it is to see an elder
face the sun
and thank God for a new day.'

'I thank God for I have my parents
and brothers and sisters alive and well.'

'I am an orphan:
I thank God for the society overseas
which sponsors my studies in this school.'

'I thank God.
for he was with me in my illness.
My family thought I would die,
but in God's mercy,
I have recovered.'

'Thank you for helping my brother
to get a job.'

'Thank you for delivering my mother
from the pains of childbirth.'

'Thank you for the sausages
we have every Wednesday.'
Limuru Girls

'Praise God for four o'clock tea,
long-sleeved blouses and brown blazers.'
Mukumu Girls

'Praise God for our science laboratories.'
Alliance Boys

'Praise God for the full moon
behind the tall trees
in our school compound.'
Kaaga Girls

'I praise you for the tarmac road
passing near my home.
We used to suffer accidents
and delays,
but today these are part of the past.
Praise God that there will be no more trekking
through the mud to the market.'

'Thank you for soap and water;
for the oil that smoothes my skin.'

'Thank you for my friends;
for their smiles and greetings.
Thank you for our Kenyan custom of shaking hands;
for every opportunity of meeting new people
and making friends.'

'I thank God that I was born
into a Christian family.'

'Thank you for all opportunities to learn more
about my people's culture,
our national heritage,
for this has deepened my insight
into your care of me from the beginning.'

'I thank God for having given me this time
to hold a pen and write my thanks.'

Personal Confessions

'I am lazy; I do not work hard enough.'

'I am a pretender;
I cannot help it.'

'I am too greedy.'

'We are always quarrelling in our community;
Help us to be united.'

'Merciful Lord,
ease the sadness in my life;
cleanse my spirit
and give me the gift of security.'

Personal Petitions

'Lord, you know that I am always sick;
this makes it hard for me to do well in my studies.
Lord, hear my prayers.'

'I pray for my father to be patient with me;
may he forget the past.
Please give him an understanding mind;
and may he return to me and to my mother's home.'

'I pray for my friends
with whom I have quarrelled.'

'Lord, my family problems affect my studies;
help me not to be overcome by worry.'

'Lord, this school is a very discouraging place
for the growth of young Christians.
We are despised and mocked;
help us to grow in faith.'

For Our Land, Our People, Our Traditions...

Our Land

Lord, you have given us our land,
and through it
you have given life.
You have made our land fertile
with green vegetables,
tea and coffee;
you have given us cattle and goats,
meat and dairy products.
This land of our ancestors
is your gift
to us.

Lord, help us to work harder,
to use what you have given
to support our growing population
and for the benefit of all our people.
Lord, hear our prayer.

Lord, we need your help
to settle disputes
over the distribution of land.
Teach us to be responsible and just.
Lord, hear our prayer.

Lord, we need your wisdom,
that our land may not be ruined
by over-cultivation,
soil-erosion,
or by pollution;
so that coming generations
may also have good harvests.
Lord, hear our prayer.

Lord, the rich variety of animal life
is also your gift to us;
it is our heritage.
Make us more responsible
in our use of Game Reserves
and National Parks,
and help us to respect the life
of all your creation.
Lord, hear our prayer.
Amen.

Thanksgiving for the Nation

For the freedom of our nation
and all the benefits of civic liberty;
for freedom of action
and the power of self-determination;
for freedom of speech and religious worship;
for freedom from persecution;
We give thanks to you O Father.

For the founder of our nation,
for the leadership of our president
and his government;
for the privilege of citizenship;
We give thanks to you O Father.

For the rapid development of industry;
for free milk and free education in primary schools;
for peace and stability
and the loyalty of our people;
We give you thanks O Father.

A Prayer for Our Nation

Lord, we pray for our nation:
for our President and his cabinet;
for all who hold authority in our land
and guide our policies,
that they may lead us
with all wisdom, justice and goodness;
that there may be true understanding
between leaders and people,
so that we may live in peace
and continue to enjoy
political and economic stability.
Lord, hear our prayer.

Lord, you understand all our ambitions
and all our problems.
Unite our people more closely
in service to one another,
that your love may be seen also
in the care of the poor
and handicapped.
Make us more aware
of each other's needs
and help us to put others first,
as you have taught us
by your own example.
Lord, hear our prayer.

Lord, help us to appreciate
the freedom and peace we have achieved
and give us strength and wisdom
to maintain it.
Let us not be separated
by tribalism,
racialism,
religious belief,

or by thoughtless action.
Help us to develop
friendships with other nations.
Lord, hear our prayer.

May the spirit of Harambee*
continue in us
as we strive
to make Kenya
a great nation.
Lord, hear our prayer.
Amen.

*See *Kenya 'Through the Looking Glass'*

Our African Heritage: A Thanksgiving

For our sense of solidarity;
for the togetherness of Kenyan family life;
for the sense of sharing;
for the coming together of family
and friends in times of sorrow,
We give thanks.

For traditional stories
which taught us the values of love and consideration;
for the love and wisdom of elders
and grandparents,
We give thanks.

For the belief of our people
that life is more than a human body,
that death is not the end;
for our faith in you as Creator
and Guide in all we do,
We give thanks.

For our African moral values;
for self-control and moral standards
in relationships between men and women
and between boys and girls,
We give thanks.

For traditional dances and songs,
feasting and happiness
and all that is good in our culture,
We give thanks.

For changes in life today;
for the education of girls;
for the way in which our Lord Jesus Christ
fulfils and perfects our African tradition;
for the churches which have been built
throughout our land,
We give thanks.

A Prayer for Our Traditions

Lord, we pray that our precious traditions
may not be forgotten;
that loyalty between husband and wife
and respect between parents and children
may continue.
Help us to obey our elders,
so that we may live in peace.
When we do wrong
help us to accept punishment
and through it to learn to do what is right,
for this is our tradition.

Lord, help us always to remember and respect
the values of our peoples;
and may we continue to have that sense of community
to make us one.

Help us to see that your will
is done today,
that no one is neglected,
so that we also may earn the respect
of future generations.

May the spirit of Harambee*
continue in us
as we strive
to make Kenya
a great people.
Amen.

* See *Kenya 'Through the Looking Glass'*.

Epilogue

Here is Good News . . .
The very Son of God became a human being,
to live among us.
The manner of his coming
surprised us . . .

We did not recognize his coming;
only some shepherds
and three mystics came from another country.
But we,
Jews, Europeans, Africans,
peoples of the world,
were not there.

He offended us.
We did not see the sign
to us and to all peoples:
the sign of an ordinary baby,
     wrapped in Jewish swaddling bands;
the sign of an African baby,
     born on banana leaves.
It was too insignificant!
But here is the gospel . . .
That the Son of God has come *down* to us,
the Word of God made flesh,
alive in the world,
full of grace and truth.

Thank God
Tony Jasper

'This is a book of meditations, thoughts. . . .
The setting is the world, life, living. That
means war, unemployment, racism, ecology.
That means falling in love, parents, clothes,
bed-sits. . . . TV, records, music. *Thank God*
is about me, you. . . .

'This book springs off one major belief: Jesus
is. Jesus is the one person who tells us about
God. He breaks through and makes sense of
ourselves. . . So let's thank God for Jesus –
here and now!'

100 Contemporary Christian Poets
Compiled by Gordon Bailey

This selection contains poems by 100
contemporary poets – some well known,
others as yet unknown. Almost all the poems
are previously unpublished.

It is not a book of 'religious' poetry, but rather
a selection of poems by Christians of widely
differing interests and experience. The variety
of ideas, subjects and styles included reflects
this diversity.